Family life

Brigid McConville

Macdonald

A MACDONALD BOOK

First published in Great Britain in 1988 by
Macdonald & Co. (Publishers) Ltd
London and Sydney
A BPCC plc company

ISBN 0 356 13736 8

Editor Donna Bailey
Production Controller Julia Mather
Picture Research Donna Thynne
Designed by Jim Weaver

Printed in Portugal by
Printer Portuguesa

Macdonald & Co. (Publishers) Ltd
Greater London House
Hampstead Road
London NW1 7QX

BRITISH LIBRARY
CATALOGUING IN PUBLICATION DATA
McConville, Brigid
Family Life. – (Children in Conflict)
1. Children and adults
I. Title II. Series
306.8'74   BF723.A33
ISBN 0-356-13736-8

Credits

The publishers would like to thank the following for use of
   their copyright material:

Andes Press Agency/Carlos Reyes: pp 17t, 33b, 35, 40b
Anna Arnone: p 7b
BPCC/Aldus Archive: p 27t
Camera Press: p 34t
Centrepoint Soho/John Goldblatt: p 26b
Denis Doran: p 18
Format: pp 15t (Sheila Gray). 34b
G.L.C. Photographic Library: p 5t
Sally & Richard Greenhill: Cover top, pp 6, 7t, 9t&b, 10,
   11t&b, 12-13, 16, 19t&b, 26, 27b, 36, 37
The Mansell Collection Limited: p 4
Network: pp 14 (Barry Lewis), 15b (Sunsil Gupta), 23
   (Chris Davies), 31b (Mike Abrahams), 33t (John
   Sturrock)
Popperfoto: p 24
Rex Features Limited: pp 12t, 21t, 25b, 28, 31t, 32, 41
Adrian Rowland: p 29l
Peter Sanders: p 39b
The Shaftesbury Society: p 5b
Frank Spooner Pictures: p 40t
John Twinning: pp 22t, 30
Zefa: pp Cover bottom, 8, 17b, 22b, 38, 39t.

Contents

Castles and cottages

What would a poor child of the past have thought of our western modern homes? Most of us have food in the fridge, hot and cold running water, TV, heating, separate bedrooms and bathrooms. But we tend to forget that these things which we take for granted are quite new – and quite rare in other parts of the world.

In past centuries, home life for ordinary working people was often very harsh. In the city slums as well as in the country cottages, whole families lived in just one or two rooms. There was no privacy. There were no plumbed-in baths or indoor toilets either.

Poverty meant that children often went without food. If they were weak, children could often die from the many diseases which modern vaccinations and medicine have almost done away with in the western world.

Yet people simply didn't expect to live for as long as they do nowadays. 'Old age' started at any time after aged thirty. Mothers died in childbirth, and marriages often lasted only a few years – because of the death of a husband or wife. If children lost both their parents and became orphans, they often faced a terrible fate. With no home of their own, they were put into workhouses and treated as slaves.

Babies and small children often died when they were little too. Families were so used to this that they would use the dead baby's name a second time around when another child was born. This was also a way of keeping a traditional family Christian name going.

Below A mother watches anxiously over her sick son. It's the beginning of this century when sick children often died at home. In slums like this, whole families often had to eat, work and sleep in the same room. It was hard to keep healthy when homes were so overcrowded and lacking in sanitation. The young girl carries on with her sewing job to earn money for the family. No matter how hard her father works as a labourer, he isn't paid enough to keep his family in comfort and good health.

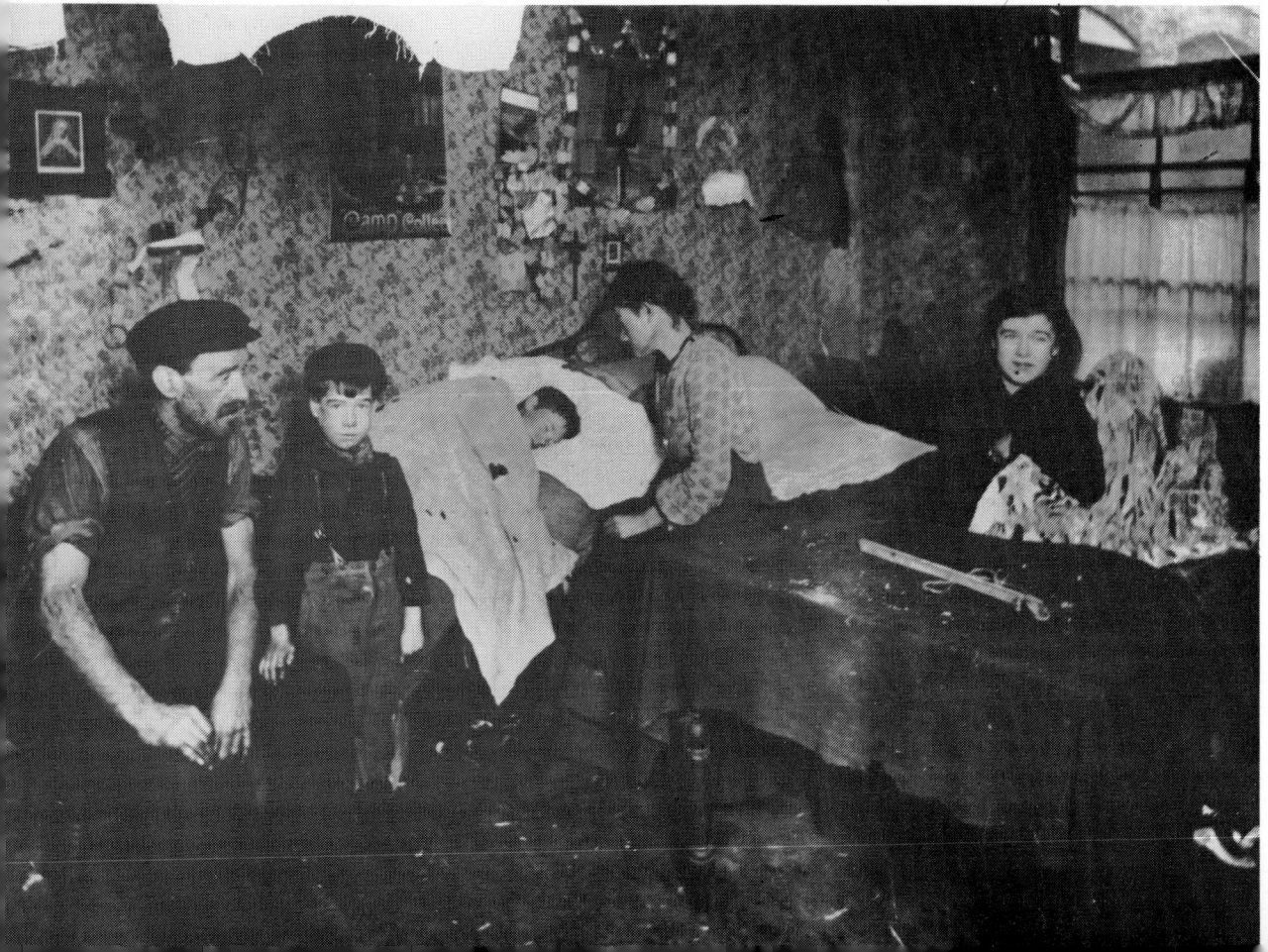

Home was also the place of work, and children had to labour with their parents from an early age. Poor children never got the chance to go to school. After the Industrial Revolution, the old home industries were taken over by big factories and children no longer worked at home. Instead, they spent most of their waking hours in factories tending machines, or down the coal mines.

But home life for upper class children was a different story. Until recent times, people didn't think of childhood as a special time of life. Instead, children were treated and dressed as small adults. Aristocratic boys studied Latin and Greek, with plenty of whippings from their tutors if they didn't pay attention. The girls were also trained in 'womanly' skills – learning to sing, to embroider and to play musical instruments for the entertainment of their future husbands. Most of this 'education' went on at home.

By Victorian times, upper class children were looked after by nannies when they were small, and then sent away to select public schools as they grew older. But the servants and the nursery remained more familiar and homelike to these children than their own parents in their elegant living rooms.

Above Home isn't just inside the four walls of a house or flat. For these Londoners, photographed in 1908, home life takes place on the doorstep and in the street, as much as in the living room or kitchen. When your front door opens straight out onto the street only a few feet from your neighbour's, it's impossible not to have a relationship with them. The children living here don't have much space to themselves – they share not only bedrooms but beds with brothers and sisters. But they do have a sense of community that today we have mostly lost.

Below This little miss isn't short of attention with two uniformed nannies to look after her. At about three years old she is as well dressed in her fine coat and boots as they will ever be. Home life for her couldn't be more different to that of the poor children of Victorian England. She lives in her own, special nursery, with staff to cater for her every need. Her parents live in a different, adults' part of the house – but they visit her in the nursery at tea-time.

Closing the ranks

Above Watching television takes up a lot of time for many children when they are at home. These children don't have to go to school for a week or so. They are at home for the Christmas holidays, relaxing with their mum and a neighbour in front of the fire. Home is where they live until their late teens or early twenties. Until then they are under the care and control of their parents. So if their mum doesn't like what's on the box, it's too bad for the children!

These days, home is perhaps the most important place in the life of a child. It's where children do most of their living and learning. True, children from about the age of five do spend a lot of time in school. But at the end of the day, they come home to do their homework and in school holidays they also stay at home.

Home is the source of every essential thing in a western child's life – food, clothing, shelter, sleep, love and affection, security. That's very different from the situation a few hundred years ago, when most children went out to work all day, or worked at home with their parents. A child caught stealing wasn't sent home to be ticked off; the young thief could be transported to Australia or even hanged!

In the modern western world, it's taken for granted that children will be at home for a longer period than ever before. This period, called 'childhood', is supposed to be a precious time for play, growing and development. Parents, as never before, are expected to help and support their children through childhood by providing a 'good home'.

In the wealthy societies of the West too, the world of work is now firmly separated from the world of home. Earning money is something that most adults do at the office or factory. And so home has become the private place for leisure and family living.

Of course there are big exceptions, such as in the developing world. There, because of poverty, not many children have the chance to be supported by parents at home, as they have to start work at an early age.

And in Britain, not all children are brought up mainly by parents at home. Take the children of the rich and privileged, who still go away from home to boarding schools to get their education. Or the children of homeless families. Or children in care, who are brought up in temporary homes or looked after by professional childcarers.

Right Playing cards with their dad is an important part of home life for this girl and her brother. These days most fathers get more time to spend at home with their kids than the working men of the past. They are more involved in the children's upbringing too. But this family are doing more than just relaxing at home. The card game helps the children learn to calculate and to concentrate. They also get to know each other better with this kind of creative play. Maybe one of them will beat their dad as well!

Above These boys leave home for most of the year to live at the expensive Harrow public school. In the public school system, children are sent away as 'boarders' from around the age of seven. They only live with their families during the holidays. It's not that different from the old upper class tradition in which tutors or nannies – not parents – bring up the children. The boys are even dressed in the formal clothes of a forgotten era, which makes them look and feel different from other children. And different from their parents pictured in the background too!

School isn't the only place where children learn things. In many ways home is a more important place for learning and developing.

Home is where children find out many vital things about themselves. They discover something that a baby doesn't know – that they are not the only person in the world. Through relationships with parents and brothers and sisters, children soon realize that they have to fit in with the needs and wants of others. And in most homes they also learn that they have a special value too.

Discipline from parents guides children as to how they should behave in the outside world. These can be hard lessons, and no child likes to be punished for what parents think of as wrongdoing. But it would be an even harder lesson to leave home thinking you can do exactly what you like, until your boss or your neighbours or the police tell you that you can't!

Learning self-discipline at home is valuable too. It's only for the first small fraction of your life that parents or teachers can order you about. For the rest of your life, it's up to you to make the most of yourself and your individual talents. You might find homework boring. But getting into the habit of working by yourself may be just as valuable to you in the future as all the information you learn in your schoolbooks.

Helping in the work of home, like washing up, tidying and keeping things clean, is also important, for boys and girls alike. Sharing and co-operating at home have their own rewards in making children feel useful and part of the family. But they are also good lessons for the future. The time comes for all of us when we don't have parents to look after our needs at home. Life can be ever so much easier for young people who know how to take care of themselves.

Below By concentrating hard on her homework, this German girl hopes to do well in her school exams. She would like to go on to college or university. But she needs peace and quiet for her studies, and her parents make sure she gets it. They want her to get on with her education while they take care of adult responsibilities, like bills and housekeeping.

Left Roasting marshmallows on the barbecue is fun. It's also part of development and growing up for these American children. They are learning how to behave as part of the family group, sharing out the food and joining in with some simple cooking. So this is quite an adventure to them, yet a safe one in the watchful presence of their dad.

Even through the kind of fun and entertainment that we have at home, children learn about the modern world. In the West, TV and radio are sources of education as well as relaxation. Playing with home computers and videos also prepares young people for a world of high technology and advanced communications.

Right High technology is now very much a part of the modern western home. This schoolboy has a whole range of computer equipment to use in his parents' study. He can do his homework, write letters or play computer games. The home computer means he is comfortable with modern communications – probably more so that his parents are!

Friends and family

For most children, home is a safe place to learn about relationships. Home is where we first feel strong emotions, where we learn to give and take love and affection. Home is also where we learn to handle anger, resentment and jealousy.

The kind of person you grow up to be depends a lot on how you get on with your family and friends. Children who grow up feeling sure that their parents love them, and that they have good friends, have the basis for loving other people when they are adults.

If you have been given plenty of love and care as a child, you are likely to be on a firm emotional footing for life. People need love to thrive, just as much as they need food. And children who grow up with a solid sense that they are worth something to their families have a better chance of bringing up their children as well-balanced people.

Having brothers and sisters can also teach children a great deal. When you argue or fight with a sibling at home, you may be getting into trouble, but you are also getting practice in how to stand up for yourself. And when you get on well with a brother or sister, when you share and help each other, you are learning how to get on with others – which will help you later in the outside world beyond home.

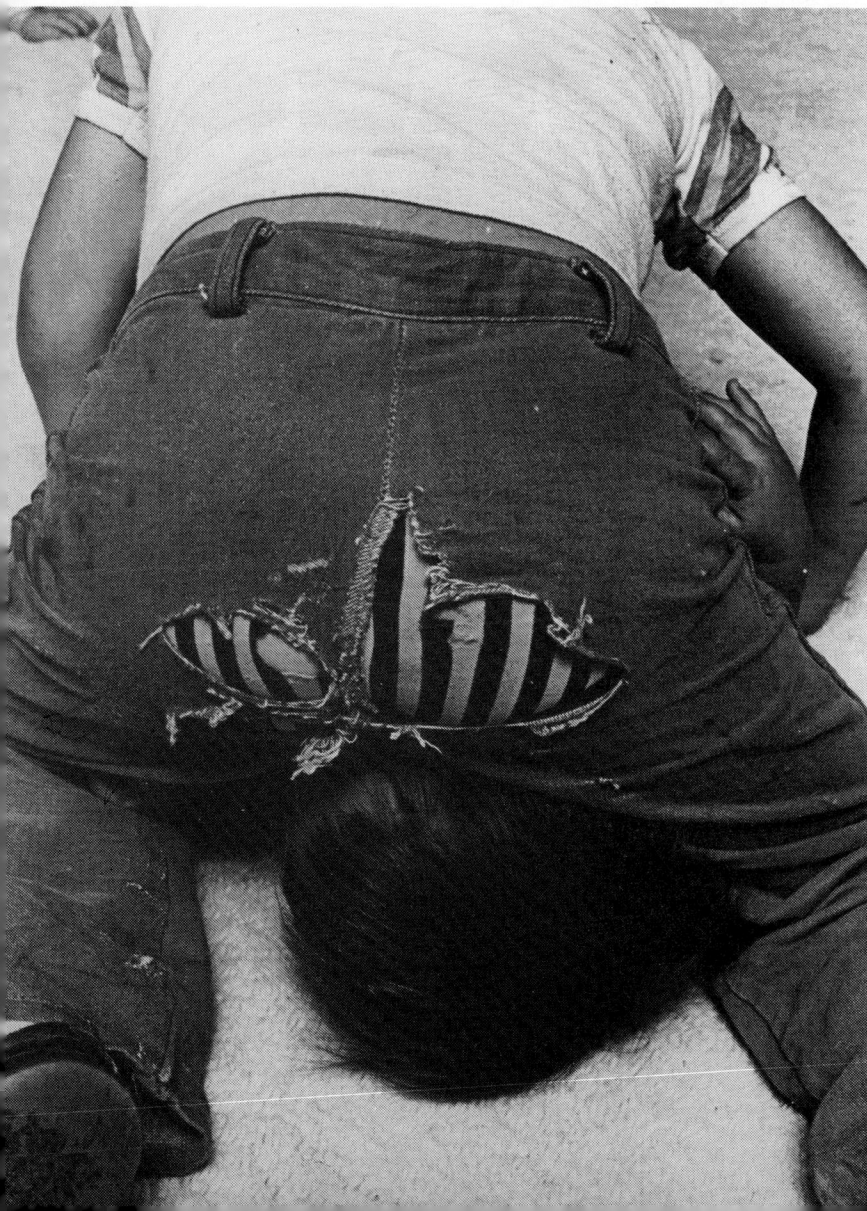

Left Is it a fight? Or is it a game? With brothers and sisters it's sometimes hard to tell. This little boy has wrestled his brother to the ground and seems to be enjoying sitting on his head. Relationships between children in the same family can be very intense. Sometimes you think you hate your brother or sister, but you can't help feeling very strongly for them at the same time. You might argue and quarrel together, but wouldn't you defend them if someone else tried to attack them?

Above Happy Birthday Tom! In celebration of the day that a new member of the family came into the world, this little boy's parents, relatives and friends have a feast in his honour. It is one day when he is the centre of attention – and his father records the occasion for the family album.

Home can also be the safe haven in which children weather the storms of their young lives. Not just adults, but children too, may have to face pain, loss, difficulty and disappointment. Death or divorce in the family can feel like the end of the world. Yet home can be the best place to find consolation and to heal the hurt.

The happy things in life are also good to share with family and friends. Birthdays, weddings and anniversaries – all are important times to celebrate as children grow up and go on to set up homes of their own.

Right These two friends are going out on their bikes. Just like adults, children benefit from and enjoy their own social life. Here, one boy has called at the home of his friend and they are deciding to go out for a cycle. From the security of home children can begin to explore the outside world, get to know each other, and become more independent.

Do parents know best?

When children come into this world they are totally dependent on adults. As babies, they can't survive unless they have a parent to love them and protect them from harm.

But from then on, there can be conflict between the child's job and the parent's job. Growing up is full-time and difficult work for a child. There is an awful lot to achieve on the road to independence, like learning to walk, to talk, to read, to get about in the world and to start forming relationships with others. The child needs a certain amount of freedom and privacy to do all this. Children have to try out all sorts of things, sometimes stumbling and getting hurt before getting it right.

A parent has a very different job – to go on caring for and protecting that child until he or she has become an independent adult. In

Above It took ages for this young woman to get her hair, make-up and clothes together this morning. She's very proud of her style. But her mum and dad hate it. They're not too keen on her boyfriend either. They think he's a bad influence, and blame him for starting her smoking. Secretly, they're terrified he'll get her involved in taking drugs. She thinks her parents are daft to be so worried.

Right Oh dear! Mum is very annoyed with her youngest child. She found her playing with a plastic carrier bag. 'You must never play with plastic bags,' she says. 'If you had put that over your head you could have suffocated!' But the child didn't mean any harm and she's crying now because her mum is so cross. Big brother looks on: at least Mum's not ticking *him* off this time!

the western world, that process can take fifteen or twenty years. Meanwhile, there can be a lot of rows and tension at home.

Parents think they know what is best for their children. They can make rules about almost everything. They ban certain television programmes. They stop children eating sweets or junk foods. They don't let their offspring smoke or drink alcohol (although they do these things themselves). They make youngsters come home at certain times from discos and parties.

Children often don't believe that these restrictions are for their own good. They think their parents are just old-fashioned. Or they've got friends who are allowed to do what they are *not* allowed to do – and they want to know why.

Some parents try to impose their prejudices on children too. They stop children from having the clothes and hairstyles they want. Others don't approve of certain friends. They don't want their children to mix with those of a different race or class or religion perhaps.

But children are people too. Children have a right to their own ideas and their own identity. Often they don't want to be protected. They want to find out for themselves. But since they don't have as much experience as adults, they might put themselves at a lot of risk without even realizing it.

So parents and children either battle it out, or they try to find a balance. Either way, it's only a matter of time before the young generation will be going through the whole process again with their own children.

Above Happy confident smiles from these three city girls as they walk home from school together. They are nearly grown up. They like clothes and (some) boys and going out. But their parents always want to know exactly where they are. Their mums warn them about strange men and rape. As for the girls, they think they're old enough to take care of themselves.

Family values

Above This is a nursery classroom in Belfast, Northern Ireland. The little girl has dressed up in a hairdresser's smock and she's about to brush and style the blonde wig. But notice that the little boys are doing something quite different – building trucks and trains. Children learn at a very early age that boys are expected to do different things in life from girls. Sometimes it's a lesson that stops them from developing to the full.

It is at home that children pick up many of their values, often without even realizing how their thinking has been shaped. Some people talk about the differences between males and females, black people and white people, as if one type of human being is born superior to another.

Even from babyhood, boys are treated differently from girls. Boy babies are given blue clothes. Girls are dressed in soft and 'feminine' pink. Boy toddlers are often allowed to be more adventurous, while girls are kept safely by their parents' side. And so boys may actually become more adventurous and girls may become more timid. Then people point out the differences and say 'it's only natural'.

The same process goes on in schools, too. Boys talk more than girls, and answer more questions in class. Because boys tend to grow up as the dominating ones, girls often do better in single sex schools. At home, boys are often given more pocket money than girls, and may be expected to do different jobs in the house.

Boys then grow up to do the more adventurous and active jobs, which are also better paid. Meanwhile girls may end up feeling they aren't worth as much as boys, and so go on to do jobs which aren't as challenging, or as well paid! Luckily, these days most parents and teachers are more aware of how the old-fashioned roles for males and females can do damage to both.

We are also more concerned about the evils of another kind of prejudice, against people of a different race. As soon as they can notice what is going on, small children absorb and copy the things their parents say and do. So if children come from a home with racist parents, they tend to behave in a racist way, until they are mature enough to think for themselves.

But some parents are now trying hard to make sure that their children do not grow up with sexist or racist values. They take care that the toys and books their children have at home encourage a wider and more positive view of the human race. They teach their children that every person in the world has an equal value and has equal rights.

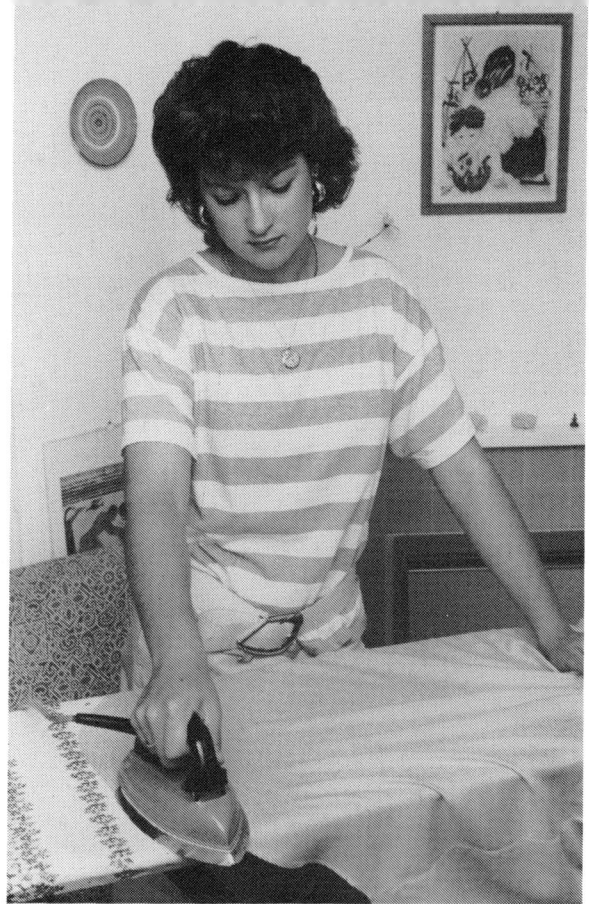

Right She looks like a very 'feminine' girl in her make-up, earrings and boutique clothes. The trouble with the 'feminine' image is that doing things like ironing may be all that girls are expected to do. And while there's no harm in a bit of ironing, or in taking care of your looks, women today say they want to be valued for their other qualities too.

Below We live in a multi-racial society. That brings a great richness to our lives, but it can also bring some tensions. In this family, the grandmother has come on a visit from India to see her daughter's family in England. Grandmother wears traditional clothes. The younger generation dress as westerners. The variety in experience, customs and ideas within this one family make home life very interesting.

Home is where the health is

What happens between the four walls of home affects your health or ill health until the end of your days.

Even before children are born, the health of their mothers and fathers influences their chances of survival. If a mother doesn't get enough to eat or can't afford medical care, her baby may be born small and sickly. Where poverty is high, the rate of baby deaths is also high. But the better off the home, the better the children's chances of fitness and health.

Parents who smoke or drink can also lead their children into habits that can be bad for health. And the simple fact of whether a home is a happy one or not is an important influence on children's mental health as they grow older.

As children grow up, their eating habits are formed at home. Some British children have chips with everything, and the traditional English breakfast is a big fry-up. But we now know that too much fat or oil in our diet is a prime cause of heart attacks.

American children tend to eat a lot of fatty foods and snacks high in refined sugar, preservatives and artificial colourings. As an experiment, one group of US pupils were switched to a healthy wholefood diet, with plenty of fresh fruit and vegetables. In a short time they went from being a school with very poor exam results to one with a very high success rate. The improved diet not only improved the children's health, but it also helped them concentrate and learn better too.

Home also affects children's health in terms of safety. It is here that a great many accidents happen. Small children are at the greatest risk of getting hurt.

Below These American children don't just eat in order to survive. They eat for fun. It's a treat for them to guzzle hamburgers and sweet fizzy drinks. But some kinds of fast food don't have many of the essential nutrients that children need for good health. It sounds ridiculous, but in rich countries like the United States there are people who suffer from malnutrition, because they eat nothing else but junk food.

When the home environment is not up to scratch, children's health can suffer in other ways. A damp house can contribute to illnesses like bronchitis. And all over the world, millions of children die because they don't have a supply of clean drinking water. As for indoor toilets and bathrooms, they are still a luxury that many people of the world can never afford.

Left South America has some of the world's poorest homes – like this one. And bad housing means bad health. In overcrowded conditions, disease can thrive, sometimes passed on by rats and other vermin. With no proper waste disposal, sanitation or washing facilities, how can a home be safe and hygienic? These children face a lifetime of bad health, if they can survive through childhood.

Below This German family goes jogging together in the park. Health and fitness have become very fashionable in recent years. While millions in the world are dying from starvation, others in the rich countries are dying from eating too much. People have begun to see that the stressful modern lifestyle, rich diet and lack of exercise is a cause of a lot of disease and death in the West.

The 'unclear family'

We hear a lot about 'the family': politicians, churches, the police – all say they're worried about what's happening to it. But aren't all families different?

Take your own family, and the families of your friends. They're not all made up of a Dad who goes out to work and Mum who stays at home to mind the two children. But many people still have a rosy picture fixed in their hearts that this is what a 'real family' should be like. Perhaps we've seen too many television shows about happy households where – despite a few hiccups – the whole fairy-tale family is always loving and loyal.

In real life, most families just aren't like that – not all the time anyway. Real Mums and Dads go through a lot of worry and stress. All parents row and get angry at times, and more and more end up getting divorced.

'Family' has different meanings to people of different races and religions. In the Far East, for instance, families tend to be much wider networks than in the West, including a range of cousins and in-laws.

A lot of children have just one parent to bring them up. (A few have none at all.) In the West, single parent families are mostly run by mothers who have lost their childrens' fathers through death, divorce or separation. Fathers, too, sometimes bring up kids without a mother in the home.

Today, it's just as likely that the mother of a European or North American family is out at work during the day, while some fathers are at home. More women are also having children without getting married or living with a man at all. Other parents are gay or lesbian.

Sometimes, divorced parents fall in love with a new partner and get married again. This can be very painful and confusing for some children who can't accept that their mother is with a man who isn't their Dad.

Or, if their father marries another woman, they worry that her rules and discipline may not be fair, or that she may not care for them. Will they be able to get on with her children? Will they feel left out or rejected if the new couple have newborn children?

These are the kinds of questions which many of today's families have to sort out for themselves. Real life may seem harder than the Happy Families fantasy, but it can also be far more challenging, interesting and rewarding.

Right This family lives in Bihar, India. With their expensive music centre and mostly western-style clothes, they are clearly well off. The stereo takes pride of place in the middle of their living room. But if western ways appeal to them more than the traditional Indian extended family, they may stick to a small, western-style nuclear family with only two children. Like people in the West, they may find they can't afford a lot of children as well as the comfortable modern lifestyle.

Right In China, a family is traditionally a much bigger group of people than in the West. Grandparents, children, brothers, sisters, in-laws and cousins all tend to grow up in the same village and keep close links with each other. Newly-weds often live with their in-laws until the older people die. Even then, the spirits of the family ancestors are treated with great reverence. But with recent laws in China to ban couples from having more than one child, the old pattern of Chinese family life is bound to change.

Left This dad has brought his toddler to the health clinic for a check-up. He could be a single parent, after his marriage or relationship with his child's mother has ended. Or he could be an 'unemployed' man, minding the child while its mother is out at work. Either way, as a parent he has got a responsible, caring and complicated job to do. There's a lot more to bringing up children than just housework!

The working mother

These days, most mothers do two jobs. One is paid – in an office, shop or factory for instance. The other is unpaid – as chief childcarer, cook and housekeeper at home.

Some women go back to paid work after having children because they enjoy 'having a job' and the satisfaction it brings. And if they earn a reasonable amount, they can usually afford to pay for someone else to care for the kids during working hours.

But a lot of mothers go back to paid work even when they don't want to, because the family wouldn't survive without the money.

There would be many more families suffering hardship if the mothers weren't bringing some kind of wage home. Single mothers usually have no choice: many have to work full time in order to keep themselves and their children out of poverty. One in seven homes in the UK is headed by a single parent, and these are mostly mothers.

A lot of women end up doing part-time work, which is often the lowest paid type of employment, because it's the only way they can work and still look after a family.

It's a big problem for most children that in the West we have a system of paid work which is designed to suit people without family duties. The nine-to-five office day is longer than the school day, so who cares for kids until a working mum gets home? There are no 'job holidays' to fit in with school holidays, so parents have to make their own childcare arrangements outside of the school term.

Good childcare, provided by sensitive and caring people, can be very good for children. They can benefit from the company of other youngsters. They can also develop loving and trusting relationships with adults other than their parents. But good childcare is expensive and often hard to find. As a result children as well as parents may suffer.

Left This woman is trying to snatch a few moments of work – but her baby isn't going to stay quiet and contented for long! Perhaps her childminder is sick today? Perhaps the baby's nursery closes before she finishes work? Perhaps she wasn't given enough maternity leave? Whatever her situation, there is almost always a conflict for mothers between paid work and caring for children. Yet most women don't have any choice in the matter. They can't afford to stop being earners just because they become mothers.

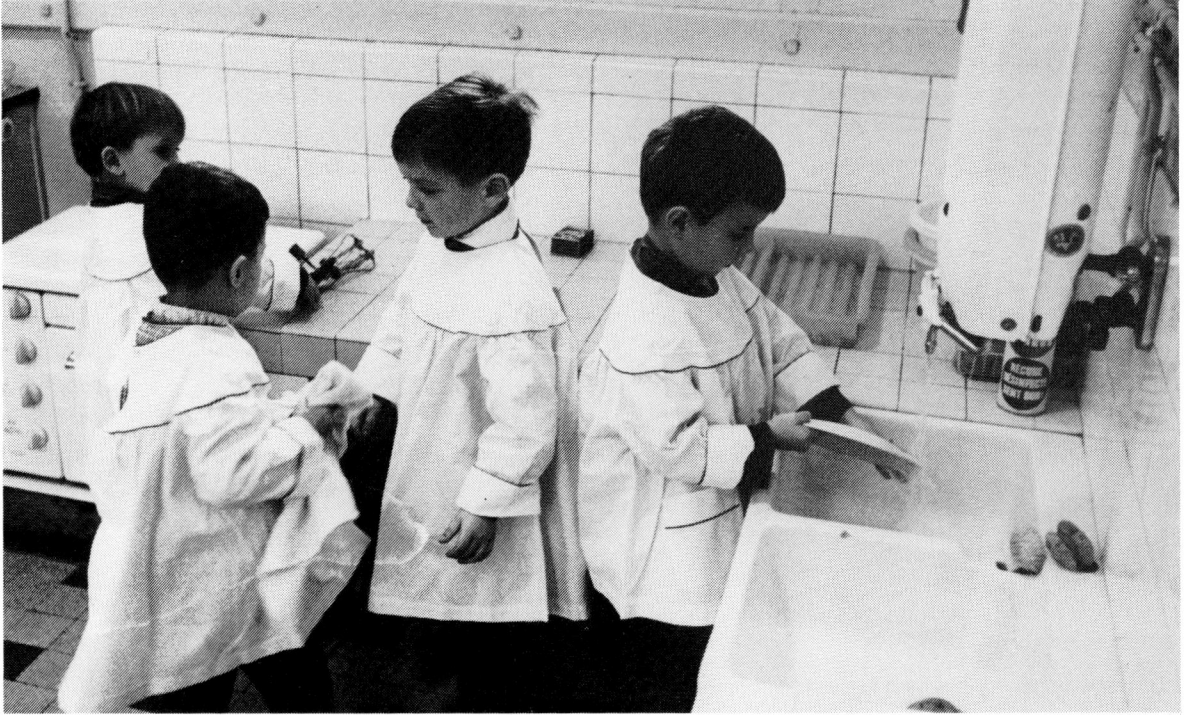

Above In France, working parents find it much easier than in the UK to find nurseries for young children. This kitchen is specially designed at a low level for small people. The little boys have put on their pinafores to do some washing up. It's a game to them, but they are also learning important lessons in helping each other and getting on together. They won't grow up with the idea that doing dishes is just a girl's job either!

Below These American children are spending most of their holidays in a summer camp. The man and woman in the picture help supervise their activities – like swinging on the rope and swimming in the lake. Most of the kids are here because their parents have to go on working even when school is closed. Maybe the children feel homesick now and then, but at least they have the chance to have a good time in the open air.

Minding the children

Above It's time to collect the baby from the childminder's home. The mum in the dark coat goes out to work for most of the day. Then she picks up her six-year-old daughter from school, and goes on to collect her one-year-old from the minder. The minder works in her own home caring for children of other women while also caring for her own daughter. It's complicated, but it's the only way these mothers can combine earning money with family life.

Some people think that little children should be at home all day with their mums. They think this is the 'right way' to bring up kids because the first three years of life are vital for a child's development.

Most mothers do stay at home when they have small babies and toddlers, and many enjoy this time very much. But today's home can be a lonely place for new parents who lack the old-fashioned social networks of friends and family in the neighbourhood. As a result, many new mothers suffer from depression, despite the joys that children can bring.

Some parents organize their own groups so that they don't have to feel stuck at home and isolated. Mothers and toddlers groups allow mothers of babies and small children to gather together for a few hours, have a chat and a coffee while keeping an eye on the children playing.

Left When children are old enough to do most things for themselves, but not old enough to be left on their own, they can be cared for by an au pair. She is a young woman from another country who lives in with the family and helps mind the children. She's not a full-time child carer, but with her help, parents can have more time to do different things.

Playgroups are for older, pre-school children who can be left for a few hours by their parents under the supervision of the adult playgroup leader. Sports and community centres may also offer 'gym tots' classes for under fives and their parents, helping small children develop physical confidence while bringing mums out of the house.

But parents with paid jobs who can't stay at home to care for their children have to find some form of organized childcare. In Britain and the US, good quality childcare is hard to find and hard to pay for. In some areas local councils provide nurseries. But these are few and far between. Usually only families in a lot of difficulty are allowed to use them.

People who work all day may take their children to a childminder's house. Childminders are professional carers who must be officially checked and put on a register with the social services. Then they can care for a small number of children at home together with their own children.

When children are happy with their minders, this arrangement can work very well. The minder's home becomes a second home to the child. And because minders have only a few children to care for, they can give their charges plenty of individual attention.

But there can be painful problems too. The 'best' way to bring up children is a very sensitive subject, and mothers and minders need to agree on this if things are to go smoothly. And sometimes children aren't happy about being left with anyone other than their own mum – which is upsetting for all concerned. Paying for a childminder can take a big chunk out of a mother's wages too.

Alternatively, in homes with enough space and money, a nanny or an au pair may come to live and to mind the children. This can work well if the nanny gets on with the family; it can be awful if she doesn't. In some jobs there is a nursery at the workplace, but these are rare and usually cost a lot. No wonder working parents often say that finding childcare is their biggest headache.

Below These toddlers spend the day in the factory creche while their mums or dads work in the factory. In this kind of workplace nursery, parents can call in to see their little ones and are nearby if a child needs some comforting. But the two nursery workers have a lot of toddlers to care for at once, and perhaps they don't all want to have a rest at the same time every day? Travelling in and out to work with parents on public transport every day is also a drawback.

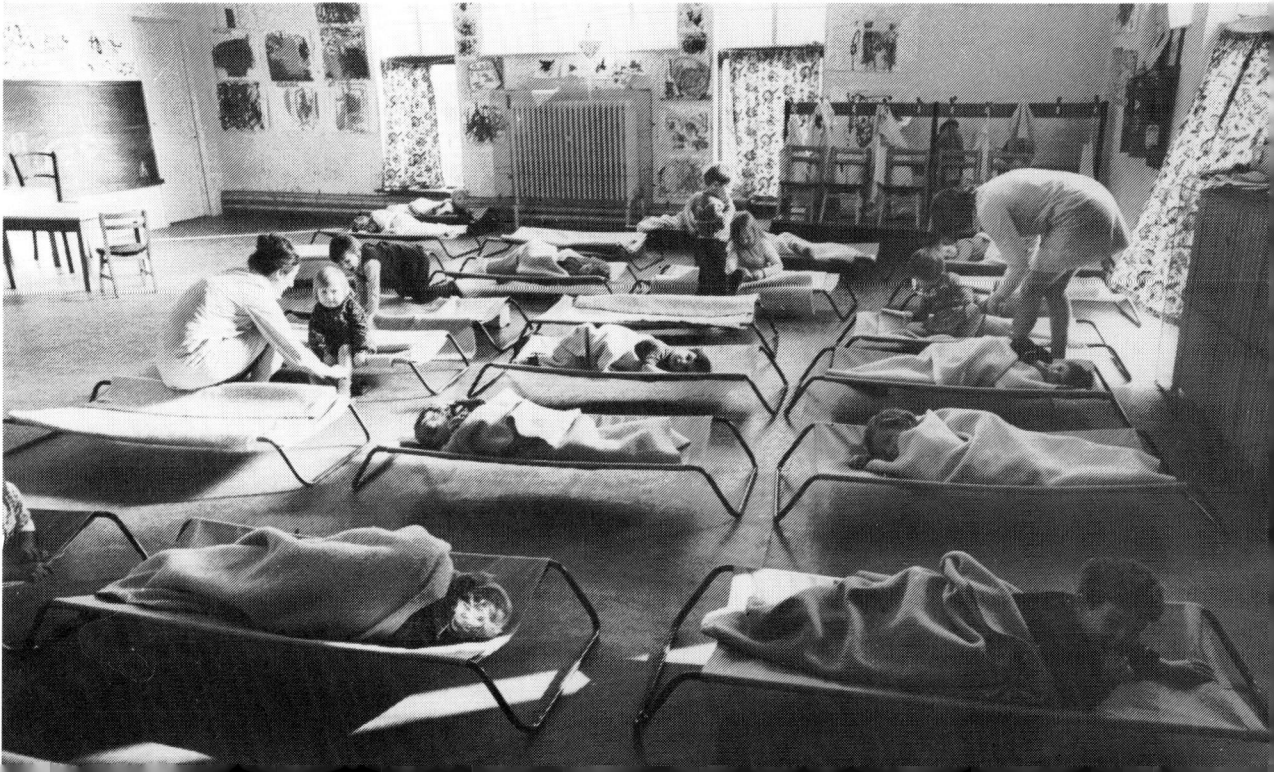

What's one of the worst things you can imagine happening in your home? Is it losing your mum or your dad? This is what a lot of children feel scared of when their parents are having rows. They are terrified that their home is going to be broken up by divorce, and that one of their parents will leave home for good.

That time on the way towards a divorce can be a long, very painful one for children as well as parents. It's horrible to see a parent you love crying and miserable. Sometimes parents can't help sharing their troubles with the children. Some will try to get the children to take sides and turn against the other parent. The tension at home can be so awful in this situation that children don't even like being at home themselves.

Sometimes one parent is always coming home drunk and getting into rows.

Sometimes men beat up their wives at home. Children lie in bed feeling terrified, listening to the shouts and bangs and crashes. At times children get caught in the middle and end up getting hit as well.

It's a common thing for children to feel as if the problems between their parents are their own fault. They don't know what they've done wrong, but they feel guilty all the same. There's almost always no good reason for feeling that way, but those guilty emotions often last a long time.

About a third of new marriages in Britain end in divorce. In America and parts of

Below We hear a lot about marriages splitting up these days but plenty of countries – like the Republic of Ireland – don't allow people to divorce. Recently there was a move to change the law so as to allow divorce in Ireland. This poster was a part of the campaign to stop that happening. But the law has not been changed, and married people stay married whether they like it or not.

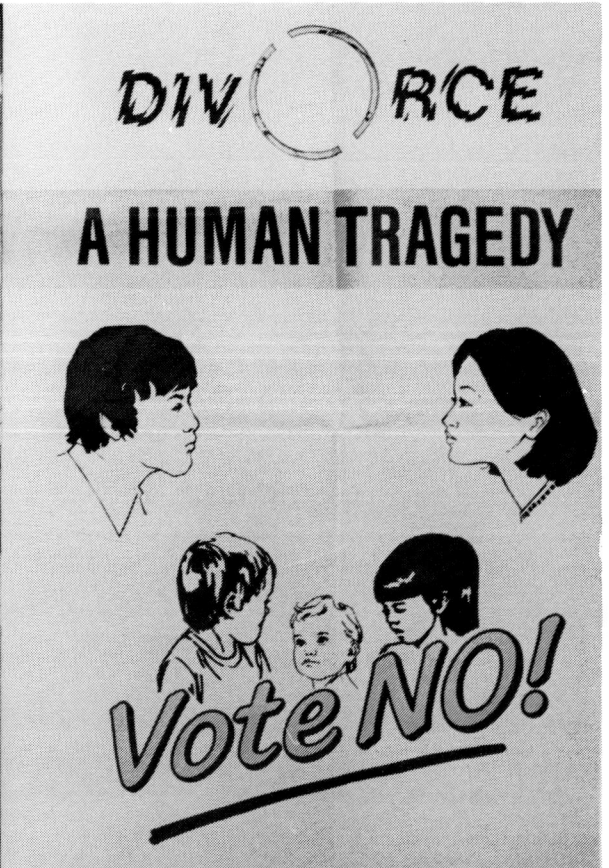

Europe the divorce rate is very high too. If that many people actually get around to splitting up, a great many more marriages must be also under strain.

But divorce is all about parents' feelings, not about children's. Sons and daughters often have no say in the matter, and no say about where or with which parent they are going to live with after the split-up. A lot of children of divorced parents also find there is a lot less money at home, as single parents often suffer financial hardship.

But there are some happy endings. Divorced parents sometimes meet new partners and the children get a new mum or dad, or even an instant family of new brothers and sisters. Sometimes the members of the family feel happier after a divorce. And in the end, time can heal a lot of the pain that comes with divorce.

Left They're at it again, shouting and yelling at each other. This little girl hates the sound of her mum and dad rowing, but she can't help listening in all the same. They act as if it's got nothing to do with her, but she worries about it constantly. She wonders if it's her fault that they are fighting, and if there is anything she can do or say to make them stop.

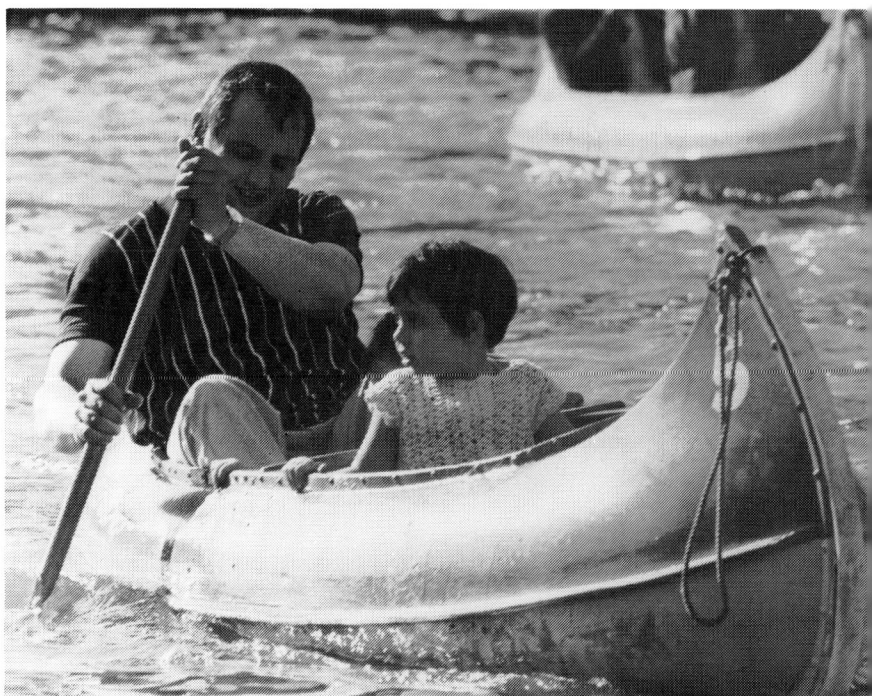

Right This American dad is divorced from his little girl's mother. But on Saturdays he takes her out for the day. Perhaps he feels a bit guilty about the divorce, because he's always doing something to try to make it up to his daughter. On this occasion it's a trip out in a canoe, and he seems to be enjoying it every bit as much as she is. She just wishes he was as nice as this when he used to live at home.

When home is not happy

Sadly, home is not always a happy place for children. Nor is it always safe.

Of course there are rows and reasons for tension in every home from time to time. Most parents punish children for being naughty, and the traditional way of doing this is with a smack. But deep down, most children know their parents still love them despite the punishment, and soon all is forgiven and forgotten.

Sometimes, however, the punishment can go too far, and a smack becomes a beating. It's easy to see the marks on a child who has been abused in this way. It's not so easy to see the pain in that child's heart.

Perhaps even more hidden away and even more hurtful to children is sexual abuse in the home. Children often feel as if this is their own fault, and that they can't tell anyone about it. But children are never to blame for sexual abuse, and these days there is help for children in this frightening situation.

So why do these dreadful things happen to children? There are all sorts of different theories, and no one can say for sure. But we can say that some things make child abuse worse, like stress in a home where husband and wife are not getting on. Money worries and unemployment can also make life very difficult for adults, and sometimes they hit out at the easiest target – the children.

The home is not a completely private place where adults can do what they like. Children don't belong to their parents. If the social services, the police, or a helping agency realize that children are being damaged at home, those children can be separated and protected from the parents who have hurt them.

These children are officially 'in care', usually in an institution such as a children's home. They may stay there until they find foster or adoption homes. They may be reunited with their families.

But while children may be better off in these alternative kinds of home, being taken away from their family home can still feel like a punishment to the child. Some people think that it is the violent or abusive parent – usually a father – who should be taken away from the family home and perhaps punished by the courts.

Britain, like America, has one of the highest recorded rates of child abuse in the world. Let's hope things are going to improve soon.

Left There is a lot of love and tenderness between this little girl and her foster mother. After fostering the child for seven years, the foster mum wanted to adopt her. But the local authority objected that a white woman should not adopt a black child. Their objections were eventually dropped and now adoption is going ahead. It's a chance of love for both of them.

It shouldn't hurt to be a child.

prevent child abuse. write: Box 2866, Chi., Ill. 60690 Ad

National Committee for Prevention of Child Abuse.   A Public Service of Outdoor Advertising & The Advertising Council

Above Violence against children can happen in any kind of home – from the richest to the poorest, anywhere in the world. Children may also be the victims of sexual abuse from adults at home. Fortunately, people are now becoming more aware of the dangers to children, and it's about time too. Recently, helping organizations like Childline have been set up in Britain to help children. As this billboard advertisement shows, America has its own problems with child abuse. They have organizations to help children too.

Right Who knows what is happening at home to make this boy so sad and withdrawn? There are all sorts of ways of abusing a child. We hear a lot about physical cruelty and sexual abuse. But emotional neglect can damage a young person too. Lack of love and affection at home can bring as much hidden, heartbreaking pain to children as any number of violent blows.

Runaways from home

You can be pretty sure that any child who runs away from home is a very unhappy child. The sad thing is that running away often makes the unhappiness worse, not better.

Children have all sorts of reasons for running away from their parents. Adults have all the power in a family, while children don't really have any. Sometimes parents treat children as if they own them, and try to force them to look or behave or think as the parents would like. Some children rebel by running away.

Other parents abuse their power over children by using violence against them or by abusing them sexually. These children

may run away in fear, thinking nothing could ever be worse than home.

The problem is that children alone, homeless and penniless in the outside world, are even more vulnerable to bad treatment. Some runaway youngsters get involved with dangerous drugs. Others are forced into the sex trade, through prostitution or pornography.

In Britain, groups like the Church of England have been setting up safe houses or refuges for runaways, to try to give children somewhere safe to stay after leaving home. These refuges allow children a chance to think things over and make their own decisions without contacting parents, police

Left In America, milk cartons like these are found on many kitchen tables. They show the pictures and descriptions of some of the thousands of children who have gone missing across the USA in recent years. Some have run away from home. Some have been kidnapped by strangers. Their families live in a state of constant worry, not knowing whether they are dead or alive.

or the social services, all of whom have the power to take the child straight home again. This system is still illegal, as the people who run refuges are supposed to contact parents or the authorities when a child turns up. But the refuges are hoping to get the law changed so that they can go on providing this service legally.

Not all children are missing from home because they ran away. Small children are sometimes stolen by adults and never seen again. In the USA, so many children have gone missing in recent years that a national campaign has been set up to help. Pictures of missing children appear on milk cartons and on television advertisements. Special computers are used to work out what children will look like now, after going missing many years ago. There has even been a drive to get all babies and children officially fingerprinted so that the police will have some help in finding them if they ever do go missing.

Left It's late at night in Piccadilly Circus, London. But these teenagers have got nowhere to go. It can be fun staying out late in the city, if you've got money and a bed to get home to. But if you've run away from home, or have been kicked out by your parents, or you simply can't afford anywhere to stay, it can be a nightmare. If she's lucky, the young woman in the picture won't be harassed by anybody. But she'll probably have to sleep on the street all the same.

Right Tense, miserable and afraid, this young woman sits alone with her thoughts. She is in the common room of the Centrepoint refuge for teenagers in London. She ran away from home to escape from conflict and unhappiness. But she doesn't know what to do next. At least she is in a safe place with a hot drink and somewhere to sleep – for the time being.

Danger: home can damage your health

In the West, children's lives centre on home. So why aren't more homes built with the needs of children in mind?

All children need a space to play in which is safe and clean. They also need exercise and fresh air. Yet the modern high-rise flats that so many city families now live in are tiny and cramped, with no access to gardens or parks. These flats may have a bit of green grass outside them. But often there is a sign saying 'No Ball Games', because the owners don't want to pay out for any broken windows.

Some city children end up playing in the streets. But when cars and lorries are driving about, children are at high risk of being run over or even killed.

And these days, city streets can be unsafe for a different reason. Some of the adults who use them may be a threat to children. Each

Above These Glasgow children are making the best of a bad job. They haven't got anywhere else to play, so they've made a game of straddling this pipe on the waste ground near their homes. It's not exactly a beauty spot, and there may be dangerous pieces of broken glass and sharp metal lying about too. They live in the blocks of flats in the background. But the flats are built without any facilities for children – no gardens and not enough space to play indoors.

year we hear of terrible tragedies, in which children are taken from the streets by strangers and molested or murdered. Street drug pushers can now be a problem too in some areas, even for very young children.

Children living in the countryside may have a healthier environment around their home, but cars and lorries in narrow country lanes are a danger. Children are also at risk from farmyard machinery. Others have drowned while playing near rivers, canals and reservoirs.

Right 'An Englishman's home is his castle' the saying goes. And these neat, well-to-do homes are all tidily separated by walls and garden gates. Net curtains stop anyone from seeing in. Home has become a very private and proud place for the British. But when the people who are selling up the house in this picture do move, how many neighbours will they know well enough to say goodbye to?

For small children, the interior of a modern western home can also be a dangerous place. Babies and toddlers just love to stick their fingers into electric sockets. They can pull irons from ironing boards onto their heads, and they can climb onto furniture which may topple over.

It's true that shops now make equipment – like stair-gates, fire-guards, and cooker guards – to keep children away from the most obvious dangers. But still, our homes are basically designed for adults to live in – and not to suit children.

Below Is this flat a happy home environment for a child to grow up in? Her mother tries her best to make it so. But although she and her baby are surrounded by people in the other flats, they have no real contact with them. From behind a glass window they can see the homes of thousands of neighbours. But they can't talk to them. The flats are designed without somewhere for the people who live here to meet and be sociable. No wonder so many young mums get ill from depression.

For richer, for poorer

Money isn't just a matter of what kind of car you have parked outside your home. For many children all over the world, it's a matter of life and death.

Bad housing, or even lack of any housing, is an international problem. Millions of families in the poor countries of the world live in houses that are literally made out of other people's rubbish. They rig up some old corrugated iron, some plastic sheeting – and that's home.

Above It's the healthy, happy outdoor life for these two girls with their pony. But keeping a pony is too expensive or too inconvenient for most homes. Apart from the cost of the animal, its feed and its equipment, you need somewhere to stable it and plenty of room for exercise. Yet if you have a house in the country and plenty of leisure time, keeping a pony is not an impossible dream.

It often happens when people move from rural areas to the big new cities of the developing world to look for work. Shanty towns spring up on waste ground of the cities as thousands of people build their makeshift shelters. After natural disasters too, like floods and earthquakes, many people are made homeless and have to make shelters out of whatever they can rescue.

The majority of the world's homes are without many of the comforts that we take for granted in the West. Everyone in the family eats, sleeps and lives in one or two rooms. In these conditions, disease travels fast, and children often die at a young age. In the world's poorest countries only half of children finish primary school. Only a quarter can get safe drinking water. And even fewer have any form of sanitation at home.

But poverty and bad housing is a problem for the children of the rich countries too. A third of British children live in homes which are on, or below, the poverty line. And every year the number of children whose homes are considered 'poor' gets bigger in the UK. Governments, of whatever political party, have failed to change this situation. The state benefits (like child benefit) which are supposed to keep children from poverty have got smaller and smaller in recent years.

Parents are often put under great stress as a result of poverty and unemployment. This can make home life very difficult and full of tension. As a result, children often suffer, particularly when their parents' marriages break down and their homes split up.

Yet for most of us in the western world, things have been getting steadily more comfortable at home. Since the Second World War, we are better off in many ways. Governments have introduced laws to improve health and diet and the quality of housing. Millions of people in Britain are now buying their own houses for the first time. Hours are spent by home owners in improving their own homes, and there has been an upsurge of interest in D.I.Y. as people modernize their houses.

Left Teresa, now aged seventeen, has always lived in this Belfast house. She shares it with her parents, brothers, sister, brother-in-law and the toddler niece she is holding in this picture. The house is due for demolition, and because of this the authorities won't do any repairs. Two years ago the ceiling fell in on the family while they were eating lunch. It was replaced, but since then some of it has fallen down again. This kitchen has none of the modern appliances that many western people now take for granted.

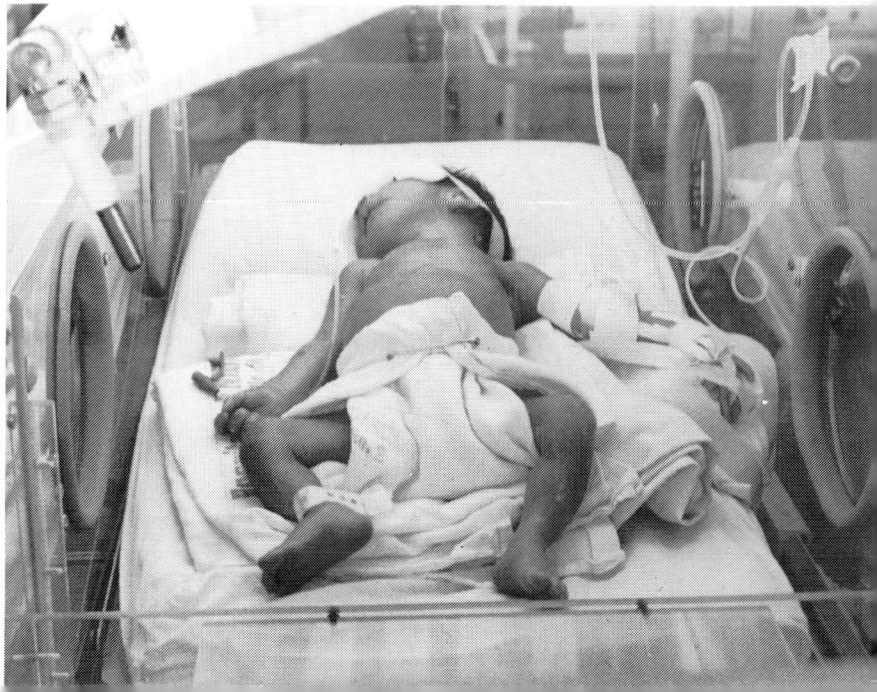

Right The ultimate price of poverty for many children is illness and death. This baby is in intensive care at the Panama City General Hospital. At home, her mother never had enough money for food, and the baby is now fighting for her life against malnutrition. In parts of the developing world, people battle not for status and success, but simply for survival.

No fixed abode

'Home' is not just a place where you live. Home has all sorts of other meanings for people.

Think of the things that you do at home, like relaxing, eating, sleeping, cleaning yourself, recovering from illness, being close to the people you love. In many ways, home is at the heart of life.

Many cultures of the world believe that home is a sacred place. In some countries, every home has its own altar and household gods to pray to. This is why losing your home can be such a terrible experience. Like an uprooted tree, families feel as if they have lost their security and their whole way of living.

Right These children have fled from their home in Kampuchea as a result of political upheaval and war. They now live in a refugee camp in Vietnam. Their new home is made of the simplest materials, but they can at least have some peace here for the time being. And that is what 'home' is all about.

Below This is Kayalitcha, on the outskirts of the South African city of Cape Town. It's now 'home' to these people. But they didn't want to come here. As part of the South African Government's policy of apartheid, the authorities forced them to leave the home they once lived in and made them settle here. But their new 'home' has nothing to offer them except one water tap in a dry wasteland.

Yet it happens all the time. Millions of children all over the world are without a permanent home because of war, famine and disaster. War and famine combined have forced the children of African countries like Ethiopia to live in vast refugee camps. These often lack any form of shelter or sanitation, and even basic water supplies.

It's not only natural disasters that make people homeless. Governments and armies are responsible for destroying homes too. In South Africa, whole settlements where black people live have been bulldozed to the ground. The families were then taken away in trucks and ordered to make new homes where the Government wanted them to live.

Many of the great political conflicts of the world have involved huge numbers of people losing – or looking for – homes. During the Second World War, millions of Jews were forced out of their homes and murdered. After that the Jewish people wanted their own homeland, which is now a country called Israel. But since then there has been conflict with the Palestinian peoples who say that *their* homes have been taken over by Israel. Now many Palestinians are living in refugee camps and a complicated struggle is still taking place.

In other countries of the world, people move their homes depending either on the seasons or the availability of work. Migrant labourers from Mexico follow the fruit harvests in America for half of the year. In Africa some tribes follow their animals from pasture to pasture as the seasons change.

In the West, there are also many children without their own homes. Every year, more and more families are made homeless through poverty. Some families in Britain end up living in bed and breakfast accommodation without the comforts and security that all of us deserve from our homes.

Below Home for these Ethiopian people is now just a patch of earth in a refugee camp. Starvation has driven them off their land. They have no roofs to cover them now: only blankets donated by a charity. Yet in the desire to call somewhere 'home' they have each marked out their own bit of bare ground with stones.

East and West

A visit to someone's home can tell you a great deal about them. If there are toys all over the place, you can tell that home life revolves around children. If there are delicate ornaments and cream carpets, you know the residents won't thank you for walking in with your wellies and muddy dog!

In the same way, homes in different parts of the world can reveal a lot about the values and way of life of people who live in other countries.

Take the European home. There is a lot of variation, depending on how much money people have got. But the 'average' house would probably have about three bedrooms, a living room, and a kitchen, plus a bathroom with toilet. Outside, there might be a smallish garden and perhaps a garage.

That tells you that European couples usually leave their parents' home when they get married in order to set up their own home. Then they have about two children and enjoy a reasonable standard of living, which is hygenic and comfortable with enough cash left over to run a car and enough leisure time for some gardening.

In the more recently established and wealthy countries like Canada, the USA and Australia, homes tend to be more luxurious.

Below There's no lack of space in this American home. It's a ranch style house spreading itself out all on one level. There's no need to build an 'upstairs' as there is plenty of land around the house. Enough land – and enough money – to build a swimming pool in the garden. But in spite of the space, there may be only two or three people living here, plus the dogs and stone rhinoceros of course!

Of course there are poor people and bad housing in these countries too. But middle class people can hope to have a swimming pool in the garden, garage space for several cars, patios for barbecues and even a second summer house by the lake or sea-shore.

Odd as it might seem, the wealthier people are, the less children they tend to have. So that you may find comfortable American homes – complete with games room or gym – with only a retired couple living there. Their two children went away to college and after that settled in a city three thousand miles away. Now they keep in touch by telephone.

Contrast this with the homes of the developing world, where most people are very poor and have many children. Again, there are exceptions, and the rich and powerful minority may live in luxurious

Above In some parts of the Far East, there is so little land available and so many people, that homes are piled up and up, higher and higher, on top of each other. There may be only a couple of rooms inside, yet three or four generations of the same Hong Kong family often live in each flat. Every single inch of space is used for something. Balconies are built out from the windows to get more space and to hang out washing, while the residents have even created pot plant gardens to make the most of their homes.

palaces. But generally, homes tend to be small and crowded. In the poorest and most heavily populated countries like Bangladesh, many members of the same family will be born, live and die on the same dirt floor.

It has been predicted that the population of the rich West will get smaller and smaller, if we don't destroy our home the planet Earth, first! Meanwhile the population of the developing world, where many homes are so poor, multiplies every year.

North and South

Climate makes a massive difference to the kinds of homes children live in all over the world. And the style of our homes also affects the way we behave and how much we mix with other people.

In the cold countries of the northern hemisphere, homes are built to protect people against the winter weather. That usually means strong walls, solid doors and glazed windows – kept firmly closed against the cold. Fires or central heating systems have to be installed. Curtains, carpets and upholstered furniture are used to keep the place snug. Where people can afford it, they insulate their lofts and double glaze their windows too. They close their curtains at night to cut out the dark and the world outside.

It all helps to keep people warm, but it also cuts them off from contact with other households. When snow and rain sends us scurrying to our separate homes, we communicate by telephone and keep in touch with the world through television, radio and newspapers.

Contrast this with the more open style of living which takes place in many of the warmer countries of the South. In a hot climate, you don't want closed doors or windows to stop the flow of air through your home. Whenever possible, you sit outdoors in a shaded courtyard, porch or verandah. Everyone else can see what you are doing and hear what you are saying. And when you share your home with a dozen relatives too, the whole family (and maybe the whole neighbourhood) is going to know each other's business!

Some parts of the world are prone to natural disasters like floods or earthquakes, and homes are built with these in mind. Japanese homes were traditionally built of light, paper-like materials. These are less likely to fall and crush the inhabitants in an earthquake. For the same reason, homes in California that are built near the earthquake zone are often only one storey high.

In other parts of the world, people build their homes with man-made disasters in mind. In Switzerland, homes are built to include nuclear bunkers in case of war.

Traditionally, people have built their homes from the most suitable materials in the regions where they lived, such as the snow igloos of the Eskimos and the leather tents of the American Indians. Where timber is in short supply, people have made their homes from stone, mud, clay, or animal dung, sometimes baked into bricks. Others have woven leaves, rushes or other vegetation to make walls or rooves of thatch.

Left The desert is a harsh environment to build a home. But these nomads of the African desert have adapted their way of life to be as comfortable as possible with the sun, sand and wind. Their roof is a tent made from animal skins. Their floor is a woven rug: no need for chairs and sofas. When they move on in search of water, the entire home can be folded up and carried with them on the backs of their animals.

But gradually the products of modern industry are replacing the old traditional materials. Instead of homes built one by one from the products of the earth, we have mass-produced homes made from concrete, glass, plastics and steel. And as these materials can now be transported anywhere in the world, modern cities with high rise buildings are springing up north and south, regardless of geography or climate.

Left This German house is designed to make the best of cold winters as well as mild summers. Notice the wide eaves of the roof. These keep the deep snow from banking up against the doors and windows of the house. Wooden shutters outside the windows can be closed to protect the house against winter storms. Yet in the summer, the wide balconies will be cool and comfortable places to sit, and the wooden troughs will be filled with flowers.

Right This Middle Eastern house is beautifully designed to protect its residents against the baking hot climate. The big, tiled courtyard and pool provide a central well of cooled air. The high stone pillars and whitewashed walls provide shade against the scorching sun. Arches and open doorways let the air circulate freely. There are no curtains or heavy upholstery to trap the heat.

Homes of the future

Ask any elderly person about home life when they were young. They will tell you what a difference modern inventions have made to the home. Electric light and power have replaced candles, gas lamps and cooking ranges. Central heating, washing machines, fridges, freezers, vacuum cleaners – home life was much harder work without them.

And technology is changing our homes faster and faster all the time. Microwaves, home computers, videos: these have changed home life even within your own lifetime.

Advances in communications could also mean more and more people working at home. Some financial whiz-kids are already 'commuting' to the office by telephone and computer links.

Other people are going to be at home with more leisure time as technology cuts down the need for human labour. And still others are going to be at home unemployed because a machine now does their job altogether.

Left In our grandparents' time, housework was a long, hard slog, with none of our modern machines to ease the burden. They could have done with some help from 'Echo' the robot. He is seen here helping his owner to load her dishwasher. Echo is just the latest in a long line of labour-saving devices that have brought a revolution to the western home in recent decades.

Right These smiling children are filling buckets with water at their new village pump in the Sudan. Until the Christian charity CAFOD provided the pump, villagers had to walk many miles to get water from a well. Now they have a clean supply of water to drink, while washing and cleaning in the home will take far less time and effort. They still don't have taps in their own homes, but they've got better water facilities now than most children in the developing world.

Left This futuristic home is called a geodesic dome. The structure is most popular in warm climates like the Middle East, the USA and Italy. Solar panels use the light of the sun to provide power for the home. It is made of light aluminium, glass and man-made fibre, with a large living space uninterrupted by pillars or walls. Some companies sell do-it-yourself kits so that people can build their own homes. And in keeping with the self-sufficiency ideal, the see-through dome makes the occupants feel they are in contact with their surrounding environment.

Changes like these could mean that children at home will see more of their parents. It has been centuries since the Industrial Revolution took 'work' out of the home. For generations now, western people have thought of 'the workplace' as somewhere – office or factory – quite separate from home.

This view of home and work is linked to traditional ideas that 'men are the breadwinners' while 'a woman's place is in the home' and 'children are dependents at home'. Perhaps in the future, if paid work returns to the home, views on these roles will be altered again?

Meanwhile, in the developing world, population growth seems likely to put even greater burdens on the homes of the world's poorest people. There are prominent politicians as well as 'alternative' minded people who are saying this situation is not only unjust, but dangerous for the whole world. They believe the developed nations have been unfairly hogging the world's resources to develop the new technology and to provide us with super-efficient homes filled with consumer devices. A worldwide movement has developed, which wants to see a fairer balance of wealth and a more natural, less technological way of life in the West.

Some people are experimenting in building homes that are more in harmony with our natural environment. American and British individuals are living in easy to build 'A-frame' houses, geodesic domes, wigwams and 'benders' made out of natural materials. These are usually cheap and free from the planning controls which cover conventional homes.

Part of the alternative ideal is to use energy which individuals can control, and which does not pollute the earth. In parts of Europe and North America, some people are turning away from electricity (which often comes from nuclear power plants). Instead they build solar panels to harness the sun's power, or windmills to bring power into their homes.

From high tech to alternative homes, from tower block to mud hut, there is perhaps more variety in homes these days than ever before in history. And as for the homes of the future: who knows what further changes time will bring?

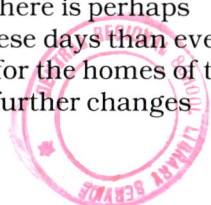

Reference

Fact file: The British home

■ In the 1980s, only 5% of households in Britain were made up of the stereotype nuclear family i.e. with a working husband, a wife who is not earning and two dependent children.

■ In 1983 only 24% of households were made up of a married couple with one or more dependent children.

■ In 27% of households there were no other family members. In another 27% of households, only a married couple were living.

■ An estimated one in eight homes is headed by a single parent – a widowed or divorced or unmarried man or woman.

■ One in ten single parents is a man – which makes 100,000 single fathers across Britain.

■ In 1987 there were 102,980 'households' (ie families or individuals needing a home) who were homeless.

■ 160,000 children a year in England and Wales experience divorce in their families. Two thirds of those are under eleven years old. One quarter are under five.

■ The numbers of children born outside of marriage has about doubled in the last ten years and is now approaching one in five of all babies.

■ One in three marriages now ends in divorce in Britain.

■ One and a half million families are on council waiting lists.

■ 11,000 people in Britain are living in bed and breakfast accommodation.

Children have rights

In their discussion paper *Children At Home*, the Children's Committee of the National Council for Civil Liberties set out what they considered to be 'a child's reasonable expectation of his or her rights' within the home. The full document is available from the NCCL (see Useful organizations) but here is a brief summary:

■ Religion and politics: 'The child has the right to freedom of thought, conscience and religion.'

■ Medical care: 'The child should have a right to overrule a parent's objection to any form of medical treatment ... i.e. an abortion.'

■ Freedom of movement: 'For the child to develop, he or she must be free to move...The tight confines of the average modern home inhibit movement, especially in high flats.'

■ The child should have the right to choose his or her friends, school and career.

■ Children should be free to express themselves, to send and receive mail unexamined, to keep diaries, to watch TV programmes (although

parents need to take care regarding horrifying material).

■ Punishment: 'The punishment of children by adults "by natural right" indicates failure to see the child as an individual...We believe all forms of physical punishment by parents should be discouraged.'

■ Pocket money: 'Children have a right to handle their own money appropriate to their needs.'

■ The child has a right to have his or her opinion respected with regard to personal appearance.

■ Cigarettes, drugs and alcohol: 'Children need protection from influences that might lead them to addiction to these.'

■ Sex: 'Complete permissiveness would be unacceptable to most children (but)...children have a right to a degree of sexual experimentation without being made to feel guilty.'

■ Privacy: Policy makers should 'begin to consider the problem of privacy...and give due weight to the particular needs of children.'

Useful organizations

The Building Centre:This is a research and resource centre which provides information about building and new materials for building homes. The Building Centre, 26 Store Street, London WC1   Tel: 01 637 1022

Child Poverty Action Group:This is a campaigning organization which works to end child poverty in Britain. One in three children in Britain now comes from a home which is on the poverty line and this situation is getting worse. The CPAG produces many publications and information leaflets, plus a journal called *Poverty*. CPAG, 1 Macklin Street, London WC2 5NH Tel: 01 242 3225

Children's Legal Centre:This independent organization was formed after the International Year of the Child. The Centre aims for the recognition of young people as individuals who need to play a full part in the decisions which affect their lives. It is chiefly concerned with law and policy and publishes the monthly magazine *Childright*, full of interesting and detailed articles on these subjects. Children's Legal Centre, 20 Compton Terrace, London N1 2UN Tel: 01 359 6251

National Centre for Alternative Technology: Provides information and advice on aspects of alternative technology – from how to build your own 'alternative' home to the various kinds of 'safe' energy. Resources include a bookshop. NCAT, The Old Quarry, Machynlleth, Powys, Wales.   Tel: 0654 2400

*National Council for Civil Liberties:*The NCCL is an independent voluntary organization protecting individual civil liberties and rights. It is a pressure group and a case-work organization providing legal advice and other services and publications. It has a Children's Committee which has produced various discussion papers (see also 'Children have rights'). NCCL, 152 Camden High Street, London NW1   Tel: 01 485 9497

*The National Children's Home:*Although most of Britain's 15 million children grow up in loving homes, many thousands of others are damaged by violence and suffering and children face the modern dangers of drugs, sexual abuse, divorce and worsening poverty. In response, the NCH has moved forward from providing residential care for children, and now has a wide variety of projects for families under stress. It publishes *Children Today*, a fact file about children in modern Britain. NCH, 85 Highbury Park, London N5 1UD Tel: 01 226 2033

National Council for One Parent Families: This pressure group represents the interests of the one in seven British families which are headed by a lone parent. One parent families are more likely to suffer from poverty than other families, and women bringing up children on their own particularly need improved childcare facilities so that they can support their families. The NCOPF helps with housing problems – amongst other services. NCOPF, 255 Kentish Town Road, London NW5 2LX   Tel: 01 267 1361

Shelter: Shelter is the National Campaign for the Homeless in Britain. They produce a wide range of published materials including periodicals, guides, reports, wallcharts, information packs and posters. They also produce audio-visual educational resources and exhibitions, factsheets, briefings and a major annual report. (See also Further reading list). 1987 was the UN International Year of Shelter for the Homeless. Shelter, 88 Old Street, London EC1V 9HU Tel: 01 253 0202

National Society for the Prevention of Cruelty to Children: The NSPCC works to prevent child cruelty and abuse and has a variety of community-based services for children and parents. They urge anyone who suspects a child is being ill-treated to contact them. NSPCC, 67 Saffron Hill, London EC1N 8RS Tel: 01 242 1626

UNICEF: The United Nation's Children's Fund, an organization which has many and various projects around the world to improve the plight of children – including their health and home life. It produces many reports and publications. UK Committee for UNICEF, 55 Lincoln's Inn Field, London WC2A 3NB   Tel: 01 405 5592

Urban Centre for Appropriate Technology: The centre has an advisory and educational function, as well as providing consultants on alternative energy – such as solar power. UCAT has set up a 'safe energy' house in Bristol, which uses safe or 'alternative energy', and which is open to visitors. UCAT, 82 Colston Street, Bristol BS1 5BB Tel: 0272 272530

Further reading

Children Today, a fact file from the National Children's Home, 1987. (See Useful organizations for contact address).

Homes Above All, by Des Wilson and Sheila McKechnie, 1986, from Shelter. Published on Shelter's twentieth anniversary, this report examines British housing conditions and policies, and argues for drastic changes in the system.

Homeless Young People in Glasgow, by Shelter Scotland, 1986, from Shelter. A report on homelessness amongst 16 and 17 year olds in Glasgow.

Make Room for Youth, by Damian Killeen, 1986, from Shelter. This report looks at why more and more young people are homeless and on the streets.

Suburban Style: The British Home 1840 – 1960, by Helena Barrett and John Phillips. Macdonald Orbis, 1987.

At What Age Can I?, from the Children's Legal Centre (see Useful organizations). A booklet which tells children what the law allows them to do and at what age.

A Child's World: A Social History of English Childhood 1800 – 1914, by James Walvin, Penguin, 1982.

The Rights of Children, edited by Robert Franklin, Blackwell, 1985. An in-depth study of children's rights today.

Index